A Map of the Island

A Map of the Island

the Island

POEMS

Nigel Darbasie

The University of Alberta Press

Published by
The University of Alberta Press
Ring House 2
Edmonton, Alberta T6G 2E1

Printed in Canada 5 4 3 2 1
Copyright © Nigel Darbasie 2001
A volume in (*cuRRents*), an interdisciplinary series. Jonathan Hart, series editor.

NATIONAL LIBRARY OF CANADA CATALOGUING IN PUBLICATION DATA

Darbasie, Nigel, (date)
    A map of the island

    Poems.
    ISBN 0–88864–371–3

    I. Title.
PS8557.A593M36 2001   C811'.54   C2001-910021-3
PR9199.3.D265M36 2001

Printed and bound in Canada by Hignell Book Printing, Ltd., Winnipeg, Manitoba.
∞ Printed on acid-free paper.
Cover painting "On the Edge of Paradise" by Doris Goudreau Darbasie. Used by permission of the artist.

The University of Alberta Press acknowledges the financial support of the Government of Canada through the Book Publishing Industry Development Program for its publishing activities. The Press also gratefully acknowledges the support received for its program from the Canada Council for the Arts.

Canada

For my father Amos, teacher and philosopher, who died on October 19, 1994; son of Robert Darbasie and Virginia Akow. For my mother Mavis who sacrificed much so that our spirits could soar; daughter of Walter Abdulah and Mildred Hughes.

Contents

Acknowledgements

My gratitude to Doris Hélène for her unfailing support.

To the Alberta Foundation for the Arts and the Canada Council for the Arts; to Leslie Vermeer, Jonathan Hart, Alan Brownoff and Cathie Crooks, my sincere thanks.

A Map of the Island

On a trip to Port of Spain
my father turned off the Eastern Main Road
into a network of San Juan back streets
where shirtless, barefooted boys scampered
and lampposts stood off-centre, in their wires
the tangled, fluttering skeletons of kites:
cocoyea frames, streamers of tail cloth.

We stopped at a two-storey house
with a side staircase leading to a veranda.
In the yard that was a patch of cleared earth
there was a woman with a broom,
sweeping puffs of dust across shadows
of breadfruit and mango trees.
I asked why we were looking at this old place.
"Because we used to live there, upstairs,"
my mother said. "That's where you were born."

3

A Map of the Island

At school, on a map of the world,
the teacher showed us home:
little more than a speck off Venezuela,
almost touching the South American coast.
Then we looked at a large map of Trinidad
and saw mountain ranges, long rivers,
the cities of Port of Spain and San Fernando,
villages and towns where nobody in class had been.

We knew that maps were deceiving.
A distance of inches down a squiggly red line
amounted to a long drive by car.
Enough time in which the land, the people,
even the air would change
and you'd be someplace different.
The teacher said that we lived on an island
but we already had proof
it was more like a vast country
where worlds lay enfolded within worlds.

4

Our Maloney Street house stood on concrete pillars
high enough for me to walk under
to the secret place I'd made
behind the back stairs. I'd look out
for scorpions and centipedes,
reddish-brown or black,
long as a finger.

Centipedes were poisonous.
They had fast batteries of legs
and flat, sinuous bodies that could hide
in the tightest spaces. If you were bitten
you'd get sick but wouldn't die.

Now if a scorpion got you, that was trouble.
At school we talked about scorpions.
You didn't have to worry about their pincers,
it was the stinger on their tail
that sent people to hospital.

But I wasn't afraid: I was king of the underworld.
With a metal bar for a sword, I ruled
my perilous empire. A patch of gloom
broken by shafts of sunlight
falling on rotten boards
and rusty paint cans.

5

On weekends my father would invite the bridge boys over.
They'd talk their strange talk: "Five spades."
"Three hearts." They'd drink *Old Oak* and *Vat 19* rum,
Johnny Walker and *Bells* Scotch whiskey.
They smoked cigarettes. I'd collect the stubs,
take them to my hiding place under the back stairs,
roll the unburnt tobacco into copybook paper.
I was always disappointed, lighting up,
that I'd never had an ecstatic rush,
just bitter choking and bleary eyes.
I sneaked out their rum and whiskey too,
liking the effervescent tingle of the chaser.
Risky experiments, troubling like a scorpion sting
to think what would happen if I got caught.

The bridge boys were negro, and Indian men;
huge, towering, most of them. Funny,
teasing, with their deep voices.
"Well, look this youngster!" they'd say.
My head in a span of thick fingers
when I didn't want to be held. When all I wanted
was just to watch, from around corners
or through the crack in the door of my room,
these men with skin from black to brown,
hair kinky to straight, lips full to thin,
noses flat to sharp. Affirmations of markings
I had learned from classmates at school.
Yet nigger, coolie, and dougla
didn't fit the bridge boys,
in whose camaraderie and worldliness
notions of tribe lay obliterated.

My father liked talking about his friends,
about the bids he and Sidney Didier had made,
playing opponents from Port of Spain to San Fernando,
trouncing them all and taking their money.
"It's just brains," Daddy would say,
how he and Sid remembered every card,
deducing the ones their opponents held
behind palisades of fingers. "Simple mathematics.
That's why you have to go to school, Junior."
And Daddy would tell us every detail,
as if Mom and I knew how to play the game.

The sessions would last through the night
in the living room. The windows open
to a chorus of cicadas and frogs,
a buzz and croak timed like clockwork.
While across the neighbourhood,
dogs barked a sporadic call and response
against the distant beat of a steelband.
Before going to bed I'd look in
on my father and his friends,
heads bowed before their cards.
A pall of smoke at the ceiling light
where moths flew in frenzied circles.

Blue Soap

Monday was laundry day.
My mother would be out early
with the scrubbing board and blue soap,
at the tub, under the tap near the back stairs.
Clothes dripping from lines and from the wire bleach.

She had other days for ironing,
cleaning the house, polishing the wood floors.
Daddy always said she was fussy about the floors.
One mop for wax, another wrapped with cloth
for working up the shine, particularly in the living room
which Mom reserved for visitors.

But Daddy's bridge boys weren't the ones she had in mind,
taking over half the house on weekends,
leaving the floors scuffed,
spotted with cigarette ash, stained
from accidental libations of whiskey and rum.
She'd get vexed too bad when she saw that.

On Sundays Mom would cook special dinners.
Crab and callaloo, rice and curried chicken,
eddoes, dasheen, sweet potatoes.
She liked baking bread and cakes,
and would make ice cream sometimes,
with a hand-churn Daddy would crank.

Whenever she got him to do chores
she'd say things like, "That's what I need,
cooperation from the man of the house."
He'd tell her not to get uppity, that she was his slave.
Mom would comeback, "This slave going to revolt
an' you'll know what happen to massa
when I put something in your food."
And they'd start heckling each other and carryin' on.

There was a mystery next door
at the old house with dark, weathered clapboards.
Narrow at the front, long through the sides,
the house stood on gnarled posts that made it seem
the entire structure was tilted.
Mr. Ellison lived there; his wife had died.
It was he and his two grown-up children
Molly and Theodore.

There was another son, Delroy,
I'd heard about but hadn't seen.
People on our street said he was in jail.
And all of us kids knew
what happened when you went there:
bread and water, the cat-o'-nine-tails,
and if you had killed anybody—the gallows.

Molly and Theodore were mysteries too.
I didn't think they were at high school or college
because they never wore uniforms.
Nor had I ever seen them dressed up
like some of the working people
who went about in the mornings and afternoons.

The side windows of the Ellison house,
the ones facing our own,
were always closed, the curtains drawn.
Sometimes their front door would be open,
the old man sitting on the step.
Through the shrubbery I could see
his head of hair, a shock of bristling silver.

Mr. Ellison didn't own a car, just a bicycle
with a generator that powered a headlamp.
He'd leave the house at night. If it was quiet
I'd hear the ticking of the sprocket,
the generator whirring against the wheel.
There was a game I'd play,
looking out, trying to catch the moment
when darkness extinguished
his lamp's thin, quivering beam.

Aladdin's

In Marine Square, Port of Spain,
there was a sporting goods store called Aladdin's.
Whenever we went to town I'd go there just to look.

Cricket bats, canvas pads and football togs
didn't interest me as much
as fishing tackle: rods, lines, hooks,
colourful spoon lures that conjured up
their large elusive catch.

Then there were guns, not just airguns,
but shotguns and sleek-looking rifles.
Model planes were even more fascinating,
some like the fighters I'd seen in movies.
Spitfires, Mustangs; line-controlled,
with little engines so they could fly.
There were model boats too,
large ones, with sails and a rudder
that worked just like the real thing.

The store wasn't far from the docks,
so that the smell of the sea
would come wafting on the breeze.
That alone was enough to stir excitement,
which made looking around Aladdin's
nothing less than complete intoxication.

We played Hollywood star boys,
going where no white man had been.
Through jungles and snow-covered pine forests,
across desert and scrub; into lands where savages lived,
far from towns and cities called civilization.
"White man come in peace," that was our line.
And if you were a Red Indian you'd say,
"White man speak with forked tongue."
As the star in a jungle adventure
you'd be bwana, massa, or sahib.
The natives would tote your supplies
and guide you through dangerous territory.
Those were the good savages,
the bad ones you'd have to fight.

13

We didn't have a pretty white missy in the cast.
Schoolgirls didn't play adventure.
And our natives weren't painted up
because playing heathen savages
really was a question of faith.
Of course we knew about God and his son Jesus.
There were pictures in school, in church,
and in our homes. Jesus was white.
Everybody worshipped Him.
At school, before going out to play,
we'd sing a song that went: "Yes, Jesus loves me.
Yes, Jesus loves me. Yes, Jesus loves me.
The Bible tells me so."

Tropical Gunslinger

I had gun fever.
A potent, lingering infection
transmitted by Hollywood and caught
around 1955 in a Trinidad cinema.
That's where I was first inspired
to mimic the crack of single rounds,
the staccato bursts of automatic fire.

Every boy learned to chant such invocations
to the magical power of bullets.
We loved their ricochet, the plumes of dust
when they hit the ground beside our hero,
droning as they tracked his dive and roll,
tearing splinters from tree trunks
as he made his zigzag run for cover.

We cheered bad guys
when they were blown off their feet,
or bullet-riddled in a slow-motion fall.
And in our re-enactments of cowboys and Indians,
lawmen and gangsters, we'd death dance
with our guns blazing.

My Diana 25 was such an awesome beauty
that I'd put her in different parts of my room
just to see how she'd look, standing in a corner
or leaning against the bookshelf.
She was long-barrelled, blue-black steel,
her stock patterned with whorls and striations.

Cocking the air rifle was ritual.
You'd strike the barrel with the palm of your hand,
disengaging the breech lock, opening the chamber.
Then you'd pull the barrel all the way down,
compressing the spring in the rifle's body
until you heard the trigger click.
Insert the pellet with its bulbous head,
close the breech and you'd be ready.

Out in the backyard I'd shoot tin cans
and blow bottles to pieces.
Then there was the first time I killed a bird,
an oriole in the coconut tree. I watched
a rivulet of blood, like a thread,
twist down its yellow plumage
while the goddess Diana
dispelled my remorse.

Digestives

My mother called them man-rats.
They came out at night, in platoons,
rustling through the bush in our backyard
on raids of the neighbouring biscuit factory.
Veteran marauders, brown fur dappled white,
trundling across open ground in a halo of flour dust.

I knew the factory watchman
and had told him about my air rifle.
He invited me over to see what I could do.
I stood in a small balcony above the loading dock,
picking my targets as they ambled across floodlit grounds,
as they dawdled beside parked delivery trucks.
I shot man-rats for so. They'd tumble over, squealing,
then right themselves and bolt into the darkness.

A few days later I saw the watchman.
"No more shootin', boy. Dead rat smelling up the place
and we can't get them out." This was exciting news—
the rifle was effective after all. I told my parents.
Mom was perturbed: "I don't want to think about it.
Lord knows where those rats ended up."
The aroma of the factory's baking wafted as usual
through the house and over the neighbourhood.
"We should try some of those new biscuits," Daddy said.

The Eastern Main Road was a tumultuous congestion:
cars, trucks, bicycles; donkey carts
driven by vendors who moved through traffic
with such assertiveness and composure
that they seemed lordly.

But the taxi driver was the undisputed king.
He fancied the British Zephyr,
bedecking it with ornaments.
Front and centre on the bonnet,
a chrome-plated bird, or bird-man,
wings outstretched in flight.
Chrome side-mirrors,
chrome badges on the grille.

Inside, brightly coloured upholstery,
sometimes velvet, with a fringe
of small pompoms.
A velvet-lined dashboard too.
And in a little sanctum there,
a good-luck charm: a cross, or chaplet
of black beads or imitation pearl.

This was the one incongruity I could find,
never having thought of taxi drivers
as deeply religious men. Then again,
I understood from the way they drove
that they needed daily contact
with the divine and the miraculous.

Because it was speed down the road,
cutting in and out of traffic. Hands flashing
fancifully adapted regulation signals
along with a universal code that conveyed routes
to curb-side passengers. All the action,
even the car itself, synchronized
to a hot calypso beat.

There was no television then, only radio
that went by the name Rediffusion.
A world, in a rectangular box with a fabric grille,
in which steel bands like Tripoli and Desperadoes played
alongside the orchestras of Count Basie and Duke Ellington.
Where Lord Melody, Lord Kitchener, and the Mighty Sparrow
jammed calypsos to ballads crooned by Nat King Cole.
Where rock 'n' roll, country 'n' western,
rhythm 'n' blues followed East Indian ragas.
Where Beethoven and Bach came within an hour
of Xavier Cugat's mambos and sambas.
Where my youthful ears heard
no incongruity or contradiction:
Only music.

Pan Yard

Some nights I'd slip out to the pan yard
even though my parents had warned
I should keep far from that place
and its ba'-john men.
I was looking for music.
My mother would say trouble,
that's what I'd really find.

The band practised under a galvanized shed,
electrical cord entwined in its bamboo rafters,
drooping light bulbs burning white.
More than a dozen men stood beneath the glare,
arms and wrists moving in unison.
Rubber-tipped sticks blending,
from the indented face of steel pans,
melody, harmony, chords, bass line.
Percussion players working up the rhythm
with tumbas, shac-shac, garachas, cowbells
and motorcar brake drums.

The arranger carried the only manuscripts.
Since none of the players could read,
he'd go round, teaching parts by rote, by ear.
Members would heckle each other
about whose head was harder than steel,
who couldn't whistle a tune, for being tone deaf.
As audience you could join the laughter,
curbing it in deference to certain bandsmen
known to be quick with knife and straight razor.
It was comforting to see those men play.
They'd smile, even dance, leading you to trust
their music's disarming power would keep you safe.

Rudolph Seetahal rode a big motorbike,
wore aviator goggles and had windblown hair.
Unique among my father's friends,
I thought he was sharp for a school teacher.
Sometimes he'd drop by with interesting things,
like the day I spied him carrying a guitar case
up the front walk of our Maloney Street house.

I watched him and my father in the living room,
waited for a lull in their ol' talk,
then with excited intrusion I asked
if Mr. Seetahal would play me a tune.
He was going to a rehearsal, he said,
turning the black case down flat,
snapping open its silver clasps to reveal
an acoustic guitar cushioned in blue velvet.

Setting the instrument on his thigh,
he slid metal picks on his right hand
as if putting on a set of claws.
Mr. Seetahal began to play,
his fingers stretching and recoiling
like some long four-legged spider,
while his clawed hand barely moved
as he filled the house with sounds
I'd never heard before,
resonating so joyfully within its walls.

School of Hard Knocks

I told my parents I loved music,
that I wanted to play the guitar.
They said I'd get a better foundation
if I started out on the piano.
They knew a good teacher, Mrs. Greaves,
classically trained, studied in England.
Some of her students had won recitals,
even had write-ups in the newspaper.

So lessons twice a week at the Greaves' house,
in the anteroom that smelled of floor polish.
The room my mother said was nicely put away:
an upright piano beside a trophy cabinet;
on the walls, photos of a young Mrs. Greaves
receiving medals, cups, plaques.

I thought I could like the piano.
If I arrived early and had to wait, I'd daydream
about playing Chopin in concert halls
full of high-society people. I also changed
into a nightclub star, enthralling audiences
with ballads and hot boogie-woogie.

Mrs. Greaves always carried a foot-rule
to re-focus errant minds, and to fix bad posture
which was the first thing she'd observe.
"Sit properly. Keep your back straight."
She'd walk behind the piano seat,
give you a poke in the ribs.

"Elbows out a little more. Curve your wrists
and don't tighten up your fingers."
Then she'd start the metronome,
the little box that induced hypnotic confusion,
reminding me how important it was
that I learn to keep proper time.

On my last music lesson I got lost
between treble and bass clefs, right hand and left,
lines and spaces, white keys and black.
"Hopeless! Hopeless! It's just not in you!" Mrs. Greaves yelled,
guillotining my fingers with her ruler
and calling off the engagement between Chopin and me.

My father and I always went together
to Da Mohammed's barbershop,
up San Juan Road,
not far from the Quayzay.
Da had been giving me a trim
ever since I had hair, my father said.
But I couldn't remember that first time.

The clapboard shop was also Da's home.
At least he seemed to live there,
perched at the roadside,
the shop's back-end supported by posts
sunk into ground that sloped through underbrush
to the banks of the San Juan River.

Da would sit in his barber chair,
reading as he waited for customers.
He would have been in his forties
and seemed as though he would remain
forever smooth-skinned, with soft hands
that smelled of talcum powder and aftershave.

"Boy, you gettin' taller every time I see you."
Da was fond of commenting on my development.
He'd drape me in his white sheet, and adjust the chair.
"They feeding you growin' mash or what?"
Then he'd start the electric shaver,
using it more than the scissors and comb,
at least when it came to me.

"One day you'll walk in here taller than your father.
I won't be able to call you Junior again."
He'd say that every time,
leaving me with a sense of loss
at my hair being sheared off. My nappy wool
lying on the barbershop floor,
mingled with my father's straight grass.

Down in the Country

I went to Presbyterian schools
where my father taught
at Charlieville and Waterloo.
Down roads that branched off
the Princess Margaret Highway
into countryside life.
Clay and thatch-palm houses.
The wealthy in two-storeyed concrete
with a galvanized roof, a balustraded porch.

Some children wore uniforms:
boys in blue shirts, khaki pants;
girls in white blouses, blue skirts,
and sneakers called washikongs.
Most students went barefooted
in whatever clothes they possessed.
But no matter who you were,
your mother swore by coconut oil.
She'd rub you down with it,
sending you off to school
all sleek and shiny.

Travelling down the Princess Margaret Highway,
leaving the Northern Range behind,
scarred, undulating at the sky's edge,
I watched the central plain open
into a checkerboard of cane fields and rice paddies,
partitioned by canals and low embankments
swept by winds that smelled of earth.

At the bridge over the Caroni
I wondered what it would be like,
taking a boat down wide muddy water,
past the bend where the river disappeared
into an ocean of tall grass
scattered with islands of bamboo.

I had grumbled about going to school.
As we drove past the fields,
my father asked if I'd prefer
a more idyllic kind of toil.
I could cut sugar cane,
load water-buffalo carts.
Come planting time
I could, with bare hands,
turn the landscape vivid green.

Schoolyard Inoculations

At school in Charlieville
there was a classmate who would tease:
"Nigger, nigger, come for roti!
All the roti done!" I knew he said it
expecting me to call him a coolie.
It was especially troubling
because I thought we were partners,
having in fact traded sandwiches for roti
in a mutually relished bargain.
We also played together at recess.
And on the day that I fell into a murky ravine,
he was among friends who pulled me out
and washed me off at the schoolyard standpipe.
Still, I thought he was a shithead
for wanting to play the game
of stinging each other with tribal cuss words,
as if that would thicken up your skin
and build your immunity.

My father was headmaster of Waterloo Presbyterian
and taught the Common Entrance Exam class.
Students from the age of eleven wrote the test,
a country-wide competition
for places at secondary schools.

"Hard work and discipline,
that's how we're going to succeed."
Daddy's exhortation. I knew it well,
despising the way it seemed to stifle and grind
the joy and wonder out of life.

Almost everyone liked my father,
his knack for explaining things
not always by the book. In a desk drawer
he kept a strap, embossed with the image of a snake.
In his absence we'd make fun,
poking it with a stick and saying it was dead.

"Some of you are non-believers
when it comes to work," my father declared,
after grading a mock exam. "Up to the board, mister."
He pointed to me. "Show us how to do this problem."
Daddy looked at my calculations. "Nonsense!"

With his left hand he caught me by the side pocket,
from his right, the snake unfurled. Cut tail!
He called on a fellow apostate
who approached as if in a trance,
writing his numbers ever so carefully.
Then, trying to distance himself from the problem,
he drifted backwards into Daddy's reach.

I was never going to speak to my father again.
When we got home I broke into tears,
telling my mother I'd gotten the strap.
"What you beat the boy for?"
She started on Daddy. I felt good about that,
until he talked her into taking his side.

"No one should envy cane farmers' children
when they turn into doctors and lawyers."
He was vexed with me. "Take a page,"
he said, "from your Waterloo chums.
They're less fortunate,
but they're more diligent."

Our class did well at the exam.
Success bringing incalculable relief,
loud talk of approaching August holidays,
and apprehensions
about starting new lives in September
at city high schools and colleges.

I caught the look on my father's face,
the beatific smile,
his perfectly contained jubilation.
It was a look that showed more readily
on the faces of visiting parents
who brought him loads of fruits and vegetables.

At home, while Mom phoned the news to relatives,
Daddy reminded me of his vindication:
"See what I told you, about hard work having its rewards."
I agreed with him, as I lifted every mango
from his Waterloo bounty, feasting
until juice ran down my elbows.

Road Crew

The Beetham was four lanes
of smooth, black-top highway
being built by the Americans.
They were easy to spot:
white men sunburnt red,
shirtless and in shorts,
directing, signalling,
driving Barber Greene pavers,
bulldozers, steamrollers.
No mistaking our fellas either:
jet black, shirtless and in shorts,
with shovels, rakes, pickaxes,
working in the trail of machines.

The Beetham Highway to Port of Spain
ran past an ancient distillery,
a hulking derelict blackened all over with grime.
Rusted pipes angled in and out, opening
into vents and chimneys that wisped and shot
steamy vapours into the air.
From its western face, the plant's outflow
drained into a canal, the stench
drifting on the wind.

The highway's southern flank was mangrove swamp,
its undergrowth of stilt roots stained by tides
lapping against a gravelled shoulder.
Across the road were mud flats.
Plovers and sandpipers gathered there
in tight, swift formations
that could at one moment skim the ground
then bank skyward in just a flash
of speckled white and grey.
But that was a closely focussed, isolated view.

Overlooking the highway
stood the hills of the Northern Range
denuded to red earth,
scarred with clapboard shacks.
There were small clusters of brick homes,
part of a housing development
that had become a symbol of hope.
Turning from the hills, one gazed ahead
into a pall of smoke rising from the city dump.
Mangrove bulldozed over with garbage.
A fetid tract of artificial land
contoured with shifting hillocks and gorges
foraged by corbeaux and vague human forms
who moved eerily through its smouldering fires.

Shanty Town, that's how everyone knew
the squatters' settlement of boxwood, cardboard,
discarded sheets of plastic and galvanize
fashioned into a sagging jumble of roadside shelters.
And if you watched the people there,
through eyes inured by looking,
you could make them meld into the highway
until everything about them
seemed as natural as the swamp,
as plovers and sandpipers
clustered on the flats.

At the entrance to Port of Spain,
off the Beetham Highway,
a lighthouse appeared in the middle of the road.
A traffic island, a landmark of the docks
and of the sprawling city north of the harbour.
The lighthouse stood beside an old wharf,
its wooden jetties sagging on waterlogged piles.

Fishing boats and barges were moored there,
alongside weather-beaten schooners
with canvas sails furled to their booms.
Barebacked crewmen worked the schooner decks,
assisting passengers who sometimes counted
chickens and goats among their possessions
of cardboard boxes and grips tied with twine.

The old wharf gave way to rows of newer buildings
overshadowed by deckhouses of ocean liners,
colourful pennants fluttering from their stays.
Passengers were tanned tourists in tropical cruise-wear,
West Indians dressed up in their Sunday best,
with nothing disreputable about their luggage.
The ships' officers and crew standing by,
radiant white from their hats to their shoes.

The Occupation

A battleship had docked at the American base in Chaguaramas,
once in a while part of their fleet would arrive
and the public allowed on board.
Traffic was lined up at the base checkpoint,
sentries scrutinizing each carload
while pointing everyone to the wharf.

Beyond the guardhouse lay American territory.
Low rectangular buildings on manicured lawns,
a remarkable tidiness everywhere.
Not even a scrap of wind-blown paper
tumbled across this roadside view
of foreign occupation.

The battleship couldn't have been missed,
the way it loomed above its moorings.
Its awesome bristle of long-barrelled cannons
rendered almost benign by the convivial saunter
of civilians across its deck. And by children, running their hands
over round-headed rivets in the ship's armour plates.

An officer answered questions from the crowd,
drawing whistles and gasps of amazement
when he pointed to hillside buildings miles away,
yet within range of the ship's guns.
"Man, the Yankee could blow up this place,"
somebody said, "is a good thing they here to protect we."

In the subsiding laughter, the talk turned to American cars.
Their six or eight cylinders beat the British four.
And who could beat American movies,
American music, sweet rhythm 'n' blues?
More rapturous still, the dream
of rum and Coca-Cola
beneath the Statue of Liberty.

From San Juan we moved to Tunapuna,
into a house at the base of a hill.
We had a Julie mango tree
other boys raided
before its fruit could ripen.
We didn't have a lawn, just weeds
left to the wet, and dry seasons.
A brick fence partly concealing
the naturalness of our yard.

Across the street, an old school
with broken windows
that neighbours would have blamed on me.
I was innocent. I swear by the hilltop church,
the bell rack off to one side.
It was a long-shot from our front porch.
Work of the devil,
but I thought it was a venial sin:
the crack of my air gun lost in blue firmament,
answered by a single chime.

The spirits of the bamboo forest saw us coming.
They were ready when we entered,
trying our utmost to be careful, stealthy.
As always, we were revealed
by thin branches that snapped like shots,
and in their echo we heard
the fluttering retreat
of mountain doves we were after.

The spirits stirred the wind.
The bamboo forest moaned,
sending its parched leaves spiralling down
with a wonderful enchantment
that drew away our passion for the hunt.

39

The market building was all roof,
the open space beneath divided into stalls.
But there wasn't enough room,
so the vendors spilled out onto the streets
with their boxes and cane baskets,
their sisal bags spread on the ground,
piled with fruits and vegetables.

Miss Edna was sitting at the usual place,
in a stained dress, her head tied with a scarf.
She had a scale in front of her, on a wooden box,
coins in a tin beside her feet, paper money
rolled and tucked into her cleavage.
"Eddoes, sweet potatoes, pigeon peas!
What you want, chile?"

I filled my mother's order, pocketed the change,
then drifted toward the smell of spicy cooking.
Roti, fried channa, pulori. Souse, a peppery stew
of pig's feet with cucumber and vegetables.
Black pudding; fresh corn, roasted or boiled.
And my favourite treats: currant rolls,
tambran balls, sugar cakes.

In another section of the market
the air smelled of fish.
Large ones of all kinds lay on counters.
Pushing through the crowd,
I touched a shark's sandpaper skin,
its rows of sharp teeth.
A fishing pirogue bobbed
at the moorings of my imagination,
and instead of returning home
I headed for the open sea.

Nothing could beat wind-ball cricket:
the bat cut from a piece of wood,
an old tennis ball with hardly any fuzz,
and for a wicket, two large pitch-oil tins
one upon the other in the middle of the street.

The true cricketers would overhand bowl,
getting the ball to spin and break,
luring the batsman to swing and miss.
While the mango pelters would release
at near invisible speed.
If their aim happened to be high,
your reflexes a little slow,
then is lash in your head.

So game in progress.
We chatting up the girls as they pass by.
"You want to play some bat 'n' ball?"
The shy ones look off and smile.
Then Gloria waltz up, sweet like hibiscus.
Eddie was the man to talk.
He tell the woman he's a cricket champion,
how she could play any time
and get a long inning or a quick knock.

She say he don't look like a champion,
like a man who could stay in the wicket.
One swing an' he out. Scandal!
Eddie in a trance; he get tootoolbay.
He supposed to be battin', but he still talking.
Raj come down and bowl. Eddie miss.
Bam! The pitch-oil tins fall.
The woman smile: "You have plenty mouth
but you is no batsman." Well all the boys in love.
Every afternoon for months is cricket
as we waiting to see nice, thick, sweet, saucy Gloria.

Repossession

Queen's Royal College occupied a city block
on a boulevard of colonial mansions.
The College's main building stood two storeys high,
symmetrical wings of blue limestone
tinted brick-red in sections, with arches,
columns, and stained-glass windows.

From the centre of the building
a clock tower rose some hundred feet,
well above the shingled roof with its small spires,
and breaking through the canopy of trees.
Along the front grounds tall palms stood watch.
Stone columns supported wide gates in an iron fence,
its uprights pointed like spears.
There were flower beds on the front lawn,
and crotons growing into a hedge of mottled leaves.

Opposite, stretched Queen's Park Savannah
under canopies of samaan, poui,
flamboyant, immortelle.
The Savannah wasn't just for strolling
but for carnival parades, kite flying,
horse racing, cricket and soccer matches.
Activities that had thinned the grass in places,
down to dusty earth.

Public works conceived in the nineteenth century,
named for Britain's Queen Victoria.
But I didn't know such things
about the landmarks of my fascination.
Nor did I have names
for the style of buildings, the awareness
of tropical Gothic as a colonial artefact.

I was without history, without names for trees
as I walked by their gnarled trunks,
the College's weathered face peering through the foliage.
How could I explain the feeling
that I was in the presence of venerable witnesses,
and that if I could possess them
I'd see what they had seen, I'd be as wise,
as near immortal as they? How could I resist
laying claim to ancient wood and stone?

Ether

I was on the comedians' list of inspirational sources,
being the longest, gangliest student in class,
with the biggest pedal extremities
shod in my Daddy's brogues
instead of fashionable pointy tips.
Needing reassurance that I might be normal
I'd go looking for Etheridge,
the sensation who stood over seven feet.
He was the tallest person I had ever seen,
incredibly frail, like a man on stilts,
with a small bespectacled head
and a voice that ranged like notes
from a double bass.

He was the hecklers' delight, even at assemblies.
They'd turn phrases in the principal's address,
like "lofty goals" and "high aspirations,"
into spontaneous jokes about Etheridge.
Laughter breaking out among six hundred boys
while Ether habitually adjusted his glasses.
Sometimes you couldn't help laughing,
relieved that he was at college.
Sorry that he wasn't in your class,
shielding you with his towering vulnerability.

In the lower forms there were alliances
of class comedians and tough boys.
Packs of a half-dozen or so
who'd slip round an unsuspecting student
and rain slaps down on his head.
The open-handed blows would fall
with a swift, rhythmic patter
to shouts of "Hail! Hail!"

But the most sadistic beatings
were inflicted with words.
Fatigue, that's what we called it
when the pack surrounded you
with potent heckling
that could make you smile
at your own dismemberment.
The revelation of quirks and foibles
you had hoped would have remained unobserved,
that you had prayed would have remained unspoken.

And when your smile collapses,
when everyone can see you've had enough,
the fatigue would become livelier.
That's when you'd have to steel yourself
against the pack's instinctive rush
to drive you into a frenzied rage,
or into tongue-tied paralysis,
with your eyes misting over.

Brio was the most feared of class comedians,
studying you down to the silliest detail.
Things like the fit of your clothes,
the contents of your lunch bag,
to say nothing of your physiognomy
and the rest of your body parts.
He was a wonderful subject himself,
wearing an expansive forehead
left by a hairline receding since puberty,
that wide-faced, beady-eyed look of a pot hound.
If he had been running the streets
Brio would be the first to bark as you went by.
He'd be the one setting off the chain reaction
that would draw the entire pack of strays down on you.

"Get up, you late!" my mother shout.
Man, I fly out of bed, don't even bathe self.
Jump in a blue shirt an khaki pants,
stuff a Johnny bake in the satchel, buss out the house
and start running down Cochrane Street.
Cross the Eastern Main Road. Hit the railway station
down by the market, lucky to catch a train,
find a window an take in some morning breeze.

Reach Port of Spain,
bounce up Horse and Roger Bannister.
"We late, boy!" Roger say, "Olympics!"
Is about three miles from the station to college.
Horse lead off tru town. We cross Marine Square,
up Frederick street. Cut tru Woodford.
As we pass by Bishop's we slow down
to watch some nice ooman
before hittin the Savannah long-stretch.
Then we hear the college clock chiming in the distance.
Well Horse and Roger start to buss dirt.
Devil take the hindmost an is me who fall back.

Pass tru the college gate,
not a blue shirt on the grounds.
Run upstairs in the third-form building.
Court in session, every man behind a desk.
Master at the front table: "You're late, boy."
"Sorry, sir. I missed the train, sir."
Master watch me good: "You look like a hooligan.
Tuck in your shirt." I check to see
two big water marks drifting from armpit to waist.
"Yuh smellin rosy too bad," somebody heckle.

Get to my place, look on the blackboard.
Is triangle inside circle with all kinda tangent.
The next thing you know, the master call my name.
"You're just in time to solve this problem."
The class quiet. I hear fellas scrambling
to find an example in the textbook.
The master declare, "I'll give you a hint:
try thinking about Pythagoras."
Well nothing change.
The problem still hard no ass,
an all that come to mind is recess.

Stone columns were stately pretensions
in the facade of the Port of Spain railway station.
Its ceiling reinforced with naked steel beams
bolted together into a framework of black ribs.
Its floor, its concrete belly, hissing with trains
absorbing and disgorging passengers
in air tinged with sulphur: burnt coal
carried on clouds of steam.

It was a dirty old place where almost everything lay
beneath a film of soot, the perennial cloak
of brick walls and ledges,
spread thick and undisturbed on rafters,
the corners and interstices
occupied by flocks of pigeons.

51

Yet the station could be alluring
if you liked watching trains and throngs of people.
Students, workers; sagas, those stylish touts,
skilled at dodging conductors and riding for free.
And you could travel on the cheap
through places unseen from asphalt roads.
The view from behind, almost a different country.

Is ol' mas' one carnival,
the best we could have fashioned
from our fathers' discarded clothes.
In fat-pants and suspenders,
felt hats at our eyebrows,
we went to the railway station,
jammin' steelband a cappella
as we headed for the city.

Almost everyone was on the hadj
to Queen's Park Savannah in Port of Spain.
Royalty, from unknown civilizations,
in silk and lamé, hobnobbed
with families of spectators
whose baskets filled our carriage
with aromas of peas and rice, and curry.

Outside the city terminus
a pack of half-naked devils descended.
Skins oily blue, and ochre.
Horned foreheads. Upturned tails
bobbing in wicked waist motion.
"Pay de devil! Pay de devil!" they chanted,
hustling purgatory dues from the crowd.

An ol' mas' band came along:
women in men's clothes,
men in diapers, sucking carnival formula
from nippled *Vat 19* and *Old Oak* rum bottles.
We revelled with them awhile
before jumpin' behind giant butterflies
all the way to the Savannah.

There, at the confluence of worlds,
fantastic creatures swarmed overhead.
And down the streets,
from the empires of imagination,
flowed waves of mortal souls
dancing in the sunlight.

Carnival and College

Hot steelbands, masqueraders in the streets
Monday and Tuesday before the start
of the Christian time of ashes.
A national fete in the face of Lent.
Catharsis before supposed fasting and restraint
coming with the dawn of Ash Wednesday.

Carnival. Two days of fantasy,
satire, absurdity. Transmutations
in everyone's grasp,
jumpin' down the road, in the wake
of mas' that left questions,
that held meanings I didn't quite understand.

Why, for instance, would people play sailors?
Because it could be cheap, better than ol' mas'
for which any old clothes would do?
You could be a flour-bag sailor
in a gunnysack outfit. Or a fancy sailor
decorated with mirrors, sequins,
braids and fluffy pompoms.

Then there was the peculiarity of sailor bands,
faces powdered or masked, imitating whites.
A satire on foreign cockswains
Port of Spain had seen so many of?
Were those showy rum-corks a delight
because in playing them you could sway
in mimicked drunkenness that could easily be real?

And who could ignore jab-jabs,
motley, colourful, wearing pointed caps,
their costumes festooned with little bells?
Variegated villains who moved through the streets,
cracking the bull whips they carried,
demanding money from terrorized spectators.

Metamorphoses outside textbooks. Yet I was glad
that carnival wasn't a subject to be crammed
when it had to be lived: seen, heard, felt,
absorbed through the senses into memory.
But the unwritten past vanishes
like a band of midnight robbers.
So tell me again, those stories of mas'.

Kalenda

Grandfather Robert held stick-fighting bouts
outside his shop on High Street,
opposite the Princes Town police station.
He sold groceries and dry goods
on one side of his place, liquor on the other.
Free rum for the stickmen.
Spectators had to buy their own.

My father remembered drums granddad kept,
that someone would beat, rousing the crowd to chant
as fighters circled each other with weapons
about the length and thickness of walking sticks
cut and trimmed, as some preferred,
from the wood of the poui tree.

There were popular stickmen and unknown aspirants
looking for adulation, for the betting money.
The winner had to crack the other fella's head,
or lather his opponent into submission.
If you needed first-aid, there was some ol' cloth
for binding wounds, and a pan
to catch your dripping blood.

Carnival, could it be
sweet scintillating epiphany
or simply just masquerade,
Trinidadians in a playful romp
among Old World, New World roots?
But how could you transmute,
even into an insect or a fish,
dance with the spirit of another
while sleeping a solipsistic slumber?

Tunapuna Walk

For Winston Maharaj

It was night-time
when backyard verdure grew phantasmal,
rustling, shimmering
in a dance with the hillside breeze.
The sagas were out
playing cards under street lamps,
talking in groups recessed in the darkness.
Disembodied voices, the red glow of cigarettes.

The asphalt road turned to gravel.
Homes grew smaller,
more wood, less brick.
Kerosene lanterns burned
alongside electric lights.
We reached Syncopator's house;
it couldn't be missed.
He owned a Hammond organ
and on this night, like almost every other,
rich, sustaining melodies swirled in welcome
through his open front door.

In the Sanctuary of the Ibis

Lal was waiting for us at the Blue River.
Narrow, placid, anything but blue,
irrigating cane and rice fields
as it flowed to the Caroni Swamp.
He started the outboard on the scow
and we were off, watched by small crabs
on mangrove-shrouded banks
and watermarked roots.
Down the riverine labyrinth,
tributaries twisting into lagoons
where shorebirds fed in the shallows.
Then the Blue opened into a vast basin
leading to another that opened to the sea.

We tied the boat to the mangrove
and cast our hand-lines.
Lal telling us stories of the swamp,
of waterbirds, alligators, prowling sharks,
the silvery tarpon called grantecai.
He reminded Winston and me
that we had to catch something, or else
he'd make us walk home.
All around, the mangrove shoreline stretched
into an expansive illusion of land.
Like verdant countryside
arrayed with deserted roads.

We had moved to Valsayn,
cosmopolitan from black to white,
into a house with so many things
I wasn't used to. Like louvres,
sliding glass doors, a covered patio
opening onto a real lawn with flower beds.

Nor was I used to hibiscus hedges
and taut, orderly chain-link
wreathed with blossoming vines.
And this time there was a view.
Not all that far away, against open sky,
stood the hills of the Northern Range.

60

Valsayn had once been crop land.
There were cane fields on its southern fringe,
coconut trees stood on its undeveloped lots.
The farmers would have come from nearby villages
of Bamboo Grove and southern Curepe
where Indian music played.

Now Valsayn drew negro workers:
carpenters, bricklayers, general labourers,
arriving on foot, on bicycles,
or squeezed together in near derelict cars.
When the houses were finished,
the women would come to cook, to clean.
The matronly and the young,
the overlooked occupants
of semi-detached servants' rooms.

Barefooted, in ol' clothes,
he'd arrive out of nowhere
to cut the grass, cleave neat edges,
tend the flower beds.
He'd slip his cutlass into the soil,
severing weeds at the roots, drawing them out,
settling the disturbed earth with his hands.
When he was through, he'd come up to the house
to rest in the shade of the carport.
My mother would bring lunch
and the money he charged.
I'd see him next down Aruac Road,
off to another job, a spectral form
shimmering in the heat waves.

Sweet Lime

We rode seven in the Blue Max, a Peugeot
Joel "Cobra" borrowed from his daddy
on Sunday afternoons
when we'd dress in fine threads,
scent our bodies with aftershave,
and head uptown in search
of whatever action we could find.

We'd cruise the Savannah.
Stop to visit Jasmine,
a friend of ours,
pass some time sitting outside
with her and her parents.
They lived just down from a club
where a jukebox would play
into the evening,
loud and ever so sweet,
A Whiter Shade of Pale.

Our classroom had been moved into the college hall
with its high ceiling of white plaster, vaulted,
ornate with tracery and hung with chandeliers.
Sunlight came through stained-glass windows,
casting dappled patterns on the wood floor
and on the wall of honour, the Great Wall,
inscribed with names of scholarship winners.
Of the list, C.L.R. James, E.E. Williams, V.S. Naipaul
stood revered, their mark on the world.
This left me and some classmates wondering
if these men had carved their names into desks.
Vandalism punishable by detention, even the cane.
Yet there was hardly a desk in college
that hadn't been etched with a roster of occupants.
So we set to work with razor blades and dividers,
with a defence that no one would have pleaded:
In the face of Cambridge exams
we had been contemplating mortality.
Slackers in the shadow of scholars,
where else could we leave our names?

63

The story leapt and crackled through college,
like fire through a dry cane field.
Classroom comedians fashioned it into broadcasts:
"Newsflash! Newsflash! Homosexual affair!
Prefects known as Dr. Head and Archie
caught in the clock tower, bullin,
as local reporters say."

Bad rake.
And it could easily have been a lie
that got the two of them
hounded for the rest of their college lives.
"Aye, buller-man!" echoing down corridors,
from classrooms of students who had taken history
and studied the Inquisition.

It had some real big brain in college,
like dem math an science men wid tick glasses,
goin roun like dey bline, beatin book fuh so,
only talkin formula an equation.
Den yuh had language men. Well dem had style.
Is highfalutin Queen's English in yuh ass,
nex minute is French an Spanish, like European.
Fellas even goin foreign embassy fuh conversational.
As if dat eh enough, de boys bussin up Latin,
translatin Cicero an all kinda ting.
An if yuh bounce dem again,
recess or lunch time, it amaze yuh
when dey drop de demotic in yuh backside
an start composin calypso.

High Noon

Blame the Latin master Scofield Pilgrim
for the Jazz Club at Queen's Royal,
the distraction it caused
in those who believed they could improvise
a future outside the curriculum
of science, languages, and modern studies. It was Sco'
encouraging lunch-time jam sessions:
Johnny Blake and Wong Moon spewing fiery riffs
that brought students rushing to the Great Hall.
And if you surveyed the talent
you'd find Mickey Maharaj, Neil Payne,
Bruce Price runnin' some chord.
Charlie Austin, the young grandmaster,
serving up the Mighty Sparrow

back-to-back with Duke Ellington
then concluding with a Stravinsky recital
in a banquet of tantalizing possibilities.

I knew Johnny Blake
from Mt. Lambert R.C. He was a friend
of a good friend, Harrison Joseph.
And I'd heard the talk about Johnny the wizard,
working obeah with his band Venus Plus X.

There were four of them on stage,
under shafts of spotlights that threw
scintillating reflections off their instruments.
And it was the sight of instruments: guitars,
amplifiers, a drum set, microphones,
that generated anticipation.
The kind easily tempered by doubt,
by dint of local origin, the absence of fame.

67

But when Venus Plus X started to play
there wasn't a person who wouldn't have sworn
that a sizzling British or American group
had stepped out of the radio.
A euphoric charge went through the crowd.
People screamed. I couldn't understand
how Johnny's voice, the harmonies,
the sound of his guitar
could cause a chilling tingle
on a sultry tropical night.
Why I kept shouting his name.

Is fete we goin to,
singin some risqué Sparrow:
"Tell yuh sister to come down here
I have a message fuh she.
Tell she I name Mr. Benwood Dick
de man from Sangre Grande.
She know me well.
I give she already oi,
she mus remember me oi.
Go on, go on,
tell she Mr. Benwood come..."

An the Boz charge up, talkin
how he go rub the boy on them tonight.
Is Cambridge Exam women we limin with
an they lookin nice too bad.
So we waitin for squeeze music
to throw some waist.
Well the women jammin fuh so,
but when fete done they cross their leg,
gone home an start beatin book.
Leave Boz talkin bout Miss Palmer,
an how all a we go dead before we get something.

68

Calypsonians were celebrating mas' in Brooklyn,
mas' in Toronto. It was the music of house parties
at which we exchanged news of friends abroad.
Families packed up, gone for good,
sending us snapshots of themselves
in London's Trafalgar Square,
or up to their arses
in Canadian snow drifts.
And so we danced
to colonization in reverse,
watching sagas come back in high fashion,
with their Yankee accents,
after two weeks' reconnoitering in New York.
Our laughter would have belied the fact
that none of us had travelled
on a jet or ocean liner.
That there was now discontent
whenever we drove along coastal roads.
It was just the sea having its way,
leading our eyes to the horizon.

NIGEL DARBASIE
was born in Trinidad, West
Indies. In 1969 he moved
to Canada, settling
in Edmonton.

Nigel's work has been
published in the collection
Last Crossing (NCI); in the
anthologies *Threshold*
(University of Alberta Press),
Going Some Place (Coteau
Books), *Fiery Spirits & Voices*,
(HarperCollins), *The Road
Home* (Reidmore Books) and
Out of Place (Coteau Books);
and in the high school textbooks *Multiculturalism* (McGraw-
Hill Ryerson), *Popular Culture* (McGraw-Hill Ryerson),
Immigrant Experiences (Harcourt Brace Canada) and
Relationships and Responsibility (Harcourt Brace Canada). His
poetry has also been broadcast on the CBC.